T0193091

ON MY WAY

A Journey Home

B R A D   H E N N A G I R

iUniverse, Inc.
Bloomington

On My Way
A Journey Home

iUniverse books may be ordered through booksellers or by contacting:

iUniverse
1663 Liberty Drive
Bloomington, IN 47403
www.iuniverse.com
1-800-Authors (1-800-288-4677)

ISBN: 978-1-4759-0566-3 (sc)
ISBN: 978-1-4759-0567-0 (ebk)

Printed in the United States of America

iUniverse rev. date: 03/16/2012

FOREWORD

I have known Brad Hennagir since 1999. I met him when my kid sister, Kate, introduced her future husband to me a week or so before their wedding. I liked Brad right from the start. He is open and honest and you never have to wonder what he is thinking, because he will tell you. He and I even have some things in common. We are the same age, we both played baseball in high school, and we both were blessed to straighten out our orneriness enough to serve voluntary missions for our church. He seemed to be on the right track and I trusted my sister's judgment, so I was happy they found each other. My sister and I share a certain type of hardheadedness, explosively passionate personalities, and an unwavering dedication to our family. She is on an admirably higher level than I in all three of these categories—especially the hardheadedness. I figured Brad knew that and was game for spending forever with her. That in itself made him a saint in my book.

Brad is the kind of guy who will do whatever he can to help anyone. In my opinion, helping others is what brings him real happiness. At a time when he and his family were just starting to regain their financial footing, they made expensive repairs to their car and drove four hundred miles to help the people of Joplin in the days right after the 2011 tornado. Immediately following the death of his mother, when most of us would have taken time for ourselves to grieve, Brad suggested that the family do a service project in honor of his mother. He and I agree on this fact: you don't worry or complain about your own woes as much if you focus on the needs of others.

I can't say that I have ever helped Brad with anything, but he helped me in ways that dramatically altered my life. When the tragedy of the terrorist attacks occurred on September 11, 2001, I was working in finance at a large company. It was a good job that provided well for my family, but I was unhappy with the constant focus on making, saving, and tracking money. I wanted to work with products or do something that made a difference in people's lives. I told Brad what I was thinking, and he suggested that I look into working for a medical device manufacturer. He didn't stop there; he went on to give me references and used his influence at work to schedule informational interviews with people who could help me start a career in the medical device industry. I now have a job that I love, and that gives me the opportunity to feel like I make a difference in someone's life every day—thanks to Brad.

It is hard for me to write about Brad without mentioning Kate. They are a true team. Their marriage is what it should be. It's not perfect, but above all else, they love each other. No matter what successes or trials they have, they are in it together. Kate, like Brad, speaks openly and honestly. She does not keep secrets and does not pull any punches when she speaks. I am Kate's only sibling, and she has never done anything but brag about Brad to me. She is not just devoted to her husband; she is wildly in love with him. Brad feels the same way toward Kate. This last Christmas, he and I spent a fair amount of time talking. He couldn't stop telling me all the wonderful things Kate does that he is impressed with. As her big brother, it gives me great comfort to know that she has found that kind of love in her life.

If you ran into Brad and his family, they would make you smile. With five kids ranging in age from four to ten, there is always a lot of activity. They get pretty loud at times, but most of the noise is laughing. As hectic as things are, you would expect Mom and Dad to be pretty worn out, but most of the time, they are the ones leading the band of laughter. If you were to take things at face value you might assume that they lead easy lives full of good fortune, but that is not the case. They have experienced family members who have passed before their time due to illness or horrific accidents. They constantly deal with a host of chronic life-threatening medical issues for Kate, Brad, and some of the children. At one point, their finances were left in ruins because they trusted someone who took advantage of them. Brad's life seems to be full of trials that would drag many of us down into depression, but he is happy and hopeful. He and his family seem to be followed by a black cloud, but they are smiling and enjoying the rain.

Brad wrote this book for the same reason he does most things—because he feels it will help others. This book will not tell you how to get rich or offer a step-by-step plan that will make you successful, but if you read carefully, it just might help you to be happy and hopeful no matter what station of life you are in.

Patrick Bull

PREFACE

I wrote this book because I feel I have something to say to the world. I tried to do it as concisely as possible, but I also wanted them to have an impact on the reader. I wrote with the busy guy's schedule in mind. I am not the only person who knows what I have to say, but I like to think that I am passing on these ideas in a nontraditional manner. The world in which we live is now fast-paced, demanding, expensive, money-driven, and quickly spinning in a flat spin that may not easily be corrected. Those who know me well have often accused me of setting out to correct the world, but that is never the case. I simply have an opinion.

Over the years I have learned that my opinion is not the same as fact. For many years, I thought mine was the only correct opinion, and because I was firm in my mind-set, I was not quick to listen to other people. I thought opposing points of view were held by "blind minds." Maybe it was age, maybe it was strife, maybe it was God, but I'm now quick to listen. Just because I listen and understand does not mean I have to agree. So what's the benefit of listening without changing my opinion? There are many benefits. If I am respectful of other people and work to understand what makes them tick, I can then understand why a situation is the way it is. This is not the only reason, but it is a good one.

I have found that in my life, I am able to emotionally and mentally cope better in situations by taking a moment to find out about people. Other people do not always want to hear me talk about myself. I know that, so I listen. I feel I can only be a better person by learning about other people. Every person in the world has something to offer, including you. Therefore, listening to other people allows us to find out where we can network our love, talents, and skills. I am not the only person in the world; my opinion is clearly not the consensus, or even the only one that matters. But I still like my voice to be heard, so why would I think that other people do not have the same or similar desires? If I take the time to hear someone, I will then be able to see what I am dealing with, and I can make a more informed and complete decision.

I liken a lot of the principles in my book to love. Love is not just for the "beautiful" people. Love is for everyone, no matter what anyone says or thinks. It is the foundation of happiness. I hope and pray that all who read this book are able to find the balance of love, happiness, and responsibility. Those are the things that will help a person to succeed in life against all the challenges he or she faces. Love, to me, is too often the first thing to go when things get tough. To me, it's like church. When the schedule gets tight, or things get tough, those are the first things eliminated from life. When we get too busy and have a lot of things to do, we skip church. When we get stressed and overwhelmed, we slow down on the love we offer to people. We quickly skip the valuable steps in life that make the world a good place and then wonder why we are not happy, and why the world feels cold. The answer is because we have made it that way. When we get stressed and stop being nice, and allow ourselves to be too busy for God, we should not wonder why there is less mercy. We have that answer. We need to remember that the past is the past. Then we must adjust for the future and make the choices that are more appropriate.

As you read through this book, keep in mind all of the blessings you have in your life. You may feel down and out, but remember a time when aid came and you were bailed out of a tough spot. Change the way you see your troubles. I did not have a lifetime on earth with my mother. Instead of feeling cheated, I changed my perception. I read a lot of scriptures; I did a lot of praying. I finally came to realize that God would not call her back until it was the right time. The right time was a time in my life when I could handle it. This does not mean it was easy or smooth for me; it just means I was able to find peace with the situation I had to face. One of the blessings I had during that time was my loving wife. I assure you, she was patient and understanding. I have had times of prosperity and times of poverty. I have been happy and unhappy. One of my favorite adages to recall is "It is better to have loved and lost than never to have loved at all." That is true from every angle of life. If we can capture true happiness even for just a moment, we will have grasped the concept of it and can then spend our lives trying to catch and hold it, sharing it with other people, and enjoying the general blessing of life. We will no longer be chasing an unknown and mysterious object—happiness.

As you remember your blessings, be grateful for them. They can be recalled in a second. As you read through my words, it is my wish that you see the message for what it is: nothing less than common words from a common guy who has been blessed with more happiness than anyone could imagine. The bottom line of my message is to keep life simple. Remember that money does not mean happiness. Live on less than you earn, hug your kids, kiss your spouse goodnight, and love your God. Love is the key in life. Show love to those you love. Help someone in need, and remember where your roots were formed. Enjoy!

INTRODUCTION

It seems as though all people are looking for the perfect thing in life as it relates to them. They are in search of the perfect song that captures their life, their being, or their problems. They have yet to see the movie that they can identify with exactly. Although they have heard great songs and seen great movies and some of them are close, none of them have that perfect essence of self-identification. So it is with books. The perfect book that captures the answers to problems, trials, and unavoidable situations has yet to be written—and the list of requirements grows each day. Millions of books, movies, songs, articles, and all other types of media have been produced to date. Oddly enough, of all that has been produced, there doesn't seem to be one thing that has just grabbed hold and provided some answers to a large majority. This does not mean that what has been produced is not good; it just has not seemed to capture the exact answers that many seek. This book was written to help people understand their dispositions in life.

I have seen a lot of things in my life, especially for my young age. I have been successful, and I have struggled as well. Above all, I recall the many blessings in my life. I can honestly say that my struggles have brought me to a true sense of what is important in life.

I was raised in West Texas, mostly, and have spent the majority of my life between Texas, New Mexico, and Oklahoma. I have a background in radiology and the various modalities in which the license has allowed me to work. The part I love about my career is to be able to help people. I love working as a clinical person, because I am in a position to do my best and perhaps offer wellness to an individual. Everyone is a loved one to someone else. As I have spent my recent life as a hospital department manager, I find the fruits of my labors are twofold. One is that I can help people learn a new talent within their fields, thus maximizing their potential. The second is that I can set the expectations of quality care.

At one point in my life, I was able to take these talents and offer the world a service through my own sort of business. I left the world of what I call W2 employment and moved into a self-sustaining business. It did not take me long to learn that some things did not work out as well as I had planned. I was the father of five children. My wife stayed at home, and we were sinking fast. We were financially failing. As we lost every dollar and material possession, and had very little coming in, my wife and I learned quickly that our resources for living consisted of God, love, and little more. We also quickly learned that was all we needed, because we had a vision in our minds and hearts.

I received an e-mail one day between Thanksgiving and Christmas. The e-mail was a response to my asking for some payments that were due to us, as we were pretty much broke. The e-mail said that there was no more money. All our bills were due, Christmas was coming, and we had spent part of the last money we had on Thanksgiving. Our children were on state health care; we had no insurance for ourselves. We were more than dirt poor. Never will I forget the scene of my beautiful wife collapsing facedown on the bed and crying, asking me what we were going to do as I read her the response to my e-mail. My heart still sinks when I recall it.

We eventually lost the home in which we lived, which had been in a sense our dream home, and we knew that there were more hard times ahead. During the following year, we lost both of our vehicles. We experienced Christmas charity a few times. Through reorganizing our life, focus, and lifestyle, we eventually ended up back on our feet. It was neither fun nor easy. Nonetheless, it was fruitful for us. We had struggles, but we also have irreplaceable memories.

As I recall, some Saturdays, even payday Saturdays, we could not afford to take the kids for a fast-food burger. We simply could not afford it. We were trying to get back on our feet. Things improved when we changed our focus. Instead of retaining the bitterness that I allowed myself to carry with me over what had happened, I changed my (and our family's) view. I now focused on the chance to start fresh. I soon took in the notion that this was a chance to start over and do what I had always wanted to do instead of trying to hang on to something I had simply fallen into over the years. I went back to school. Just like a new high school graduate, I changed my major a few times. I learned a lot of things, studied a lot of different professions, but still eventually ended up back in health care. I suppose that is because that is where my love is in life—helping people.

My dear wife stood by me every step of the way. I worked a full-time job, starting work early every day. From work, I would go to class, get home as late as ten at night, and still have homework remaining. I remember getting home late one night, with a ton of homework to be done, reading to do, and a paper to write. I came in the house and it was cleaned and comfortable. The children were in bed. I missed them because I couldn't recall the last time I had spent any time with them during the week. I was starving and it had been a long day. When I saw my wife, my eyes lit up. It was the warmest greeting. She knew I was tired, burned out, frustrated, and more. I set my bag down, forgot about homework, and ate cereal as I spent time with her. It was then that I realized what means the most in life. I really beat myself up emotionally a million times over failing my wife with the unsuccessful business attempt. I felt she deserved more. I was right that she deserves nice things, but "nice things" are more than material objects. I have always wanted to provide a nice home and lifestyle. What I have learned is that in order to complete a nice lifestyle, a person needs to revere the important people in his life. My wife always believed in me, even when

I didn't believe in myself. She watched me decide to change careers after ten years in a field that I had always deemed my calling. She also watched me come back to it when I started getting on my feet emotionally. There is no doubt those times were tough.

One thing that we maintained was the love and support of God. We kept Him with us. We included Him in all we did. We taught those things to our children. It is my hope that this book will demonstrate my perspective in life. This is the perspective that kept my wife and me grounded as we got through some times that I hope and pray people never have to experience. We maintained our standards and love, and exercised faith and hope. I feel strongly that things prevailed for me because I never completely lost sight of what was important. I also feel very strongly that if I had been able to stay strong when I was weak, things would have gone more smoothly. Nonetheless, the weak moments made me stronger, and for my strength I am ever grateful.

CHAPTER 1

THINK IT, SAY IT, DO IT

It doesn't matter where it all began. We are in an active part of our lives right now, whether we like where we are or not. There is no such thing as a get-rich-quick plan. There is no millionaire waiting in the wings to give you his fortune. There is no person in the world with enough talent that people line up to give him or her money. There is always exchange for goods in the world.

While it is true that we can reach any level we seek and can accomplish any dream we have created, we must understand that this will come only through effort, sacrifice, and perseverance. We have to apply ourselves, simultaneously keeping in mind what is real. Then we can begin to enjoy the fruits of our labor—success!

Let's answer the first question. What is realistic? The answer is simple: anything. Whatever is dreamed or desired is real. It really is that simple. Part of reality is order. We simply need to understand order. Reality is order. Have you ever been in a situation where things were so loud you could not even hear yourself think? For me, that is daily life; therefore I am forced almost daily to operate on an as-needed basis. There are messes, arguments, dirty laundry, dirty dishes, and many other things that stress most people. Heck, I have five children, my wife and I are both students, and I work full-time. That is enough to choke a horse. However stressed you may feel just reading that, it is really quite relaxing. I am around children in my life. Therefore I am forced to think of nothing but fun and use my imagination all day long. I often find myself on the way to a serious engagement for work, still thinking about childlike things, as those are typically the most recent items in my short-term memory. I have no problem with that, because it keeps me connected.

What I always want to remember is that children are dreamers. They are the ones who can imagine it all and still think it is possible. Adults are commonly guilty of ruining dreams in the name of reason and reality. What would happen if we didn't exchange a dream for what we call reality? I vividly remember having dreamed up a recipe for chewing gum when I was a child. My mother never would give me the opportunity to experiment with the idea. Thus I never knew if the recipe would or would not work. Chances are strong that the recipe would not have worked very well, but if I had been allowed to experiment, it could very well have triggered something else down the road. Fast forwarding to my adulthood, I took a traveling job one time. My children were all very young. The apartment at which I stayed was a second-floor apartment. I had taken my mountain bike with me to help the time pass in the absence of my family. One weekend, my wife surprised me with a visit. When we got to the apartment, my son saw my bicycle locked to the gate on the rail upstairs. He immediately asked me if I rode my bike up and down the stairs. I thought it was funny and giggled, but I was also reminded that a child sees all things as a real opportunity. As adults, we cloud and destroy that opportunity.

I love that children are often called stars. This is so true. Anything is possible. Adults become negative and ruin the opportunity to make the unimaginable manifest. We tell children from the time they are born they can do anything they want to do—nothing is impossible. The ironic thing is that adults don't believe it. How long will it be in the life of a person before he learns that the idea of limitless possibility is a farce? The truth is we need to be like children. We need to be stars. We need to believe our own advice and practice what we preach.

CHAPTER 2

WHAT DO YOU WANT?

When I was a traditional college student, I saw a lot of "old" people in my class. The truth is that these people were not really old; they were just older than I was and more established. But they were not afraid to go back to school. At that time, online classes, a variety of night classes, and other ways for nontraditional students to earn a degree or start a new career were not around. These individuals had to really want it. Many of the classes were offered during business hours. Being a parent and breadwinner had to be shuffled. These people had to work twice as hard and struggle twice as much as their younger classmates. This was the sacrifice made for an education. As more people showed this commitment, their prayers were answered. Today, because of these people and their commitment, we are surrounded with opportunities for nontraditional students to pursue higher education. When they did it, there were so few of them that they stuck out a little.

Aside from material sacrifices, I'm sure they endured a little emotional sacrifice as well. We now we have a myriad of opportunities for higher education. Many schools are now focused on nontraditional students, and traditional schools have opened their doors in a like manner.

This is not to say that nontraditional students did not occur before my time. I'm just saying that there are many ways to progress as a result of these people. What they did for themselves eventually helped many people. What I learned is that it is never too late. My children used to go to a doctor that had gone to medical school when he was in his forties. Because of his example, I was once again reminded to never stop trying for what I want. I have been to school many times and won't stop until my goal is reached. I personally feel that a nontraditional student is a better learner. This person has been through the school of life a little bit and has a true desire to learn—and an even truer desire to succeed and make something happen when he applies himself. There is a little more maturity to bring to an education. At the same time, we need traditional students, because the creativity and energy of youth brings the feeling of limitless possibility that adults lose over time. The key is balance.

One of my favorite things is the key of balance as described by Aristotle. My paraphrase (he words it better) is that too much of anything is not right. He mentions that self-control is in itself the reward of self-control. Therefore facing a challenge eliminates fear. Indulging in the passions in a limitless manner is a faulty ethic, but not indulging in passions is also a faulty ethic. The right thing is the balance of control and emotions. If a challenge is faced without fear, the person has found the right ethic. The word Aristotle uses is "right". What is right?

My point is that there is a balance in life. There is balance in education. There is balance in the workplace. To define right is not easy; it does not come by consensus. Not everyone will agree. The quest is to answer one's own heart. What do I want? If I had my preferred way in life; what would it be? Why do I want what I want? These are questions that many people do not answer because they are afraid of themselves.

I have spent a long time researching people and emotions. People do not like what they have become inside themselves. They shelter themselves from the truth by becoming occupied with things that take their minds off of what most bothers them. For example, a person who has cheated on a spouse may become preoccupied with work. A selfish and lazy person may mask his or her shortcomings with excuses of being busy and having a crowded schedule. The people guilty of this are often quick to point out those patterns in other people. Why do they hide it? Facts are facts. The truth is that no one wants to admit when he or she does these things because they are embarrassing. I would be very surprised if I went into work tomorrow and one of my team members or employees openly admitted they wanted to do nothing but surf the Internet and collect a paycheck at the end of the day; therefore they hide out and dump assigned work on other people. The process behind it is simple to me. It makes sense. I have said and done things in my life that are embarrassing for me to even recall; I certainly do not want to announce to anyone what I did. Therefore it is natural to place it as far back in my mind as possible, as if it never happened. However, I try to remember the feeling I had when I did the embarrassing things so that I remember not to say or do those things again. The balance is to be honest about things and accept what I have done or said and learn from the experience.

Knowing what we know in life, we tend to expect outcomes to be negative. We base every decision we make on failures with an occasional success blended in the mix. We have allowed ourselves to expect the worst. I always go back to the mind of a child. If a child learns that saying "please" and "thank you" gets him a cup of chocolate milk, he will continue to do that. By the same token, he also learns that throwing a fit will get a toy removed from his toybox; he will eventually correlate the two and stop. We are all like Pavlov's dog. We correlate information. Unfortunately, as we grow and "mature," we change correlations from good to bad. We spend the majority of our lives preventing bad things from happening, instead of making good things happen. All that is required to make a difference is a shift in mentality and behavior. The question we should ask every morning when we get out of bed is, "What am I going to do to make my life better?"

I have spent many years of my life doing the opposite. I would complain because my day started way too early. I would complain because I was too tired, I had too much to do, or I had something going on that distracted me from the focus of my job. All along, I was not seeing the forest for the trees. I had all of these opportunities for success and happiness placed before me. I went to school to learn a trade that provided stability for me and my family. It afforded me a home, clothes, and the means to support and raise my children. There is no need for me to compare with someone who has more money, fewer kids to provide for, or both. There is no need for jealousy to rear its head and make me want a new car. There is no need for these things. The thing I was missing was that I have great things in my life. Life does offer rewards for comparison. The benchmark needs to be set as we reach goals. If we set a goal, we reach it. When that goal is set, we set another goal. If our goals are set and centered around what other people have, then we will never find true success because we are dedicating ourselves to living the lives of other people. We will then miss out on our own lives, because we are trying to live someone else's life. Somehow we have convinced ourselves that we are not happy with the people we are in life. Therefore we think that another way, or another item, or even another activity will bring us the link to happiness that we do not have. We just need to be ourselves as we seek happiness. The rest will fall into place if we allow it.

CHAPTER 3

LIFE IS TOUGH;
STOP BEING NEGATIVE

As I look at life from a Christian perspective, it makes even more sense. Many of Christ's teachings were geared to and about children. He loves them. He often taught them. I feel strongly that he did this because he knew they get the big picture. Our children will become what we show them they can become. Where does the responsibility really lie? Does anything help to teach more than an example? All of the teachings of Jesus are centered around happiness and worth, not wealth or self-interest. The world teaches us that wealth and self are important, and we take the bait—hook, line, and sinker. What are we doing to strengthen ourselves emotionally and spiritually, and bolster our self-worth?

I often ask myself a few questions: What would it be like to meet myself? Am I following my heart? How do I really feel? Do I really enjoy the life I am living? If not, what would change it? I use these questions as markers in my life. That is where I find my success. I have been both well off and very much the opposite. I can honestly say that I have had more than memorable times at both ends of the spectrum—and in between. Like anyone else, I would rather not be financially struggling, but when I was, I still found value and happiness in my life. However, I know all a person can do is change the position in which he sits. That is what I did. I made up my mind what I wanted and I went for it at full speed. It did not happen overnight. I'm not sure that I am where I want to be yet, but I am still trying and I know I will make it happen. I am sharing this book with the world because the precepts helped me. The purpose of a life should not be centered on money, material objects, or greedy behaviors. It should be centered on happiness. The desire of the heart is where happiness is found. Balance in all is the key to success and happiness. A person needs money, love, and more. To balance them all is the secret to life. The balance requires service to other people, love of one's self, love of other people, and the opportunity to take a chance every once in a while. Without a challenge, we cannot grow.

I went through a time in my life where I was challenged greatly, beyond anything I would have ever imagined. Having learned a few things along the way, I now see why I encountered what I did. At one point I thought I was being cruelly punished by God for being a bad person, even though I had never really thought I was one. I lost my home, my cars, my retirement, and much, much more in a worldly sense. Eventually, I got it back through God, the support of a loving wife, and hard work. It was tough. During the period when my finances were going through "reconstruction," someone stole from my bank account. At the same time, I was in the process of paying back taxes. That is a small glimpse of what I went through. When I refer to "I," I mean I, my wife, and our five children. My children were young. We experienced a charity Christmas and many more things that came with love from other people. As we moved past those times, I have kept in mind to pass it along and never forget.

During those times, my wife and I also had a serious look at our relationship. Those times were tough on us, and they caused strain. We were never in jeopardy of losing the relationship; the tough times just caused us to take a look at ourselves and see where we could be even stronger. What I learned is that some of the behaviors we had formed during the good times caused strain, and could not continue through the hard times. One thing I learned is that it easy to take blessings for granted when times are good. The blessing in this is love. We learned where the damage was originating and exactly what was wrong. The question was never our love for each other, but our situation was a call to action.

It goes back to what I like to call the "wake up question." What am I going to do to make my life better? I did not ask myself this every day in our relationship. If I was all that my wife ever talked about (in a good way), what am I doing that is causing that? Have I ever stopped doing that? An even bigger question is do I love her so much that she is all I ever talk about? Certainly I love her that much, but love is also an action word. I need to do more than talk about it; I need to show her. I need to do things in my life that let her know I love her. I also need to be aware of the times she needs me—and then be there for her. I'm not saying what happened during those times were fatal, immoral, or otherwise. They were cause for bettering my life. The struggles of those years have caused us to cross and build bridges in our relationship that have made us stronger. I like to think we have always had an ideal marriage and relationship. The struggles of a painful life overhaul have caused us to be even stronger. I love the times I have with her, just as I love the times I have with the children we have made.

I have learned that there is such a thing as balance in all things. Wealth does not always mean more problems. A person does not have to poor to be happy. I think every person needs to read the New Testament, even those who are not Christian. There is so much about life in there and lessons that everyone in the world could use. I feel that if people work too hard to make life good, they are missing the key. Here is the way I see it. Imagine a beautiful home. Now imagine you want to go inside, so you kick the door in. From that time on, instead of fixing the door, you just lean it up against the doorway, blocking out most of the elements. All along, you were never aware the key was under the mat. That is what I feel many people are doing with their lives. While the majority of things are figured out, the one thing they want is right in front of them—and they are not aware of it. It is just a matter of small application. I love the simple things in life that the New Testament tells us made Jesus happy as he spread the Word to other people. He served people. He taught people. He never had any of the finer things. As a matter of fact, He only received a gift of some of the finer things after he was dead; they were a gift from Joseph of Arimathea. This does not mean, to me, that we must not be allowed anything nice during our lives on earth. To me this means our focus should be on the balance of happiness in life. These things come from service, love, and a focus on the things we cherish and revere.

CHAPTER 4

PUT THE RIGHT THINGS IN YOUR LIFE

As we go through life, we form relationships of all sorts. We have friends, work friends, acquaintances, etc. We also have the people we interact with on a deeper level, dear ones such as spouses, significant others, children, and other family. What are we doing to tie those binds tighter? Do we get mad at the people we are not close to and take it out on the ones we are? I have been guilty of that. I have found that if we do things that way, it is a sure recipe for disaster. My personal experience has also been that if I get mad and lose my temper in any situation, I then have strong feelings of remorse. If we stick up for ourselves in a calm and respectful manner, more people will listen and cooperate. The result is almost always a compromise. If a person is always bending, it is not fair. Let me explain.

In a situation of difference, there is always a person who "loses" (for lack of a better word). In order to prevent an argument, the person who does not like contention usually concedes and takes the short straw. As time passes, this person becomes tired of the situation and wants out. When anything that might cause confrontation arises, this person responds by telling him—or herself that the other person will get mad and it is not worth it. My clear and lucid response to this pattern of behavior is that the situation is never going to stop and you need to stop allowing it to happen. It is your fault, because you won't take a stand. You deserve to be happy. You deserve for people to put themselves out for you. In a situation of difference, it only seems as though someone will always have to make the sacrifice. My question to you is this: Why are you always choosing to be that person? Why can't it be someone else? The bottom line is that you need to face the fear and take a stand. People will treat you the way you let them. The real way to look at the situation is that there is compromise in all things and you need not always take the hit and absorb the unhappiness. If you take the stand, other people will respect you and know that you require compromise and you expect respect.

As we form relationships in life, we need to remember to surround ourselves with people who bolster us as we return the favor. No true friend always takes. Service equals happiness. Have you ever been talking to a friend and felt wonderful after the conversation is over? That's person we all need to be. That's the feeling that can happen every day in life if we allow it. We need to eliminate the "can't" from our lives. The world has taken a turn down Easy Street. What we have forgotten is that Easy Street is not in a nice neighborhood. It is full of incomplete tasks and poorly kept commitments. I like to see the good in people—and then focus on it. As people see the good and improve it, the things that need attention quickly become noticed and get attention as well. The same is true for all people.

If we follow this process, it does not mean we will avoid struggles in life. It doesn't mean that we will find wealth, love, and free time in a week. It means we know where to find the things we need. More importantly, it tells us how to find what we need in life. It will help us find the answers to the things we need to make our lives happy. Not every job is made for all people. If that were true we would all be engineers or doctors. The world is varied for a reason. We are all a piece to a puzzle. When we work together to fit together, the big picture is clear. It is full and complete. We become greater when we do our part to make other people greater. As we learn to identify what we need in life, we then know what we need to get. When we get what we need, we are lifted up and able to help other people do the same. As we help other people, we are then lifted further. Other people begin to follow suit and a circle of success is the result. The first step in making all of this happen is to change the way we think. We need to get back to the basics. We need to focus on the results of successful efforts instead of expected failures. Is the glass half empty or half full? Neither—it's a glass of milk which we are glad to have, with room for more. Changing the way we look at things allows us to change the way we seek things. Changing the way we seek things allows us to attain things.

Again, we need to get ourselves back to the way a child thinks. Anything is possible, even for an adult. We can go back to school, we can change careers, and we can make anything happen. The first step is dreaming, and the next is believing (in yourself). Then you will make the dream come true.

As a child, I would stand at the end of the dirt road and hit rocks from it into a field. I would stare at the clouds in amazement, peeking over them to see if I could see God, or my great-grandmother who had recently passed away. I hang on to this memory, because it allows me to remember my foundation in life. Like anyone else, I started out with much to learn. What I forgot was to dream along the way while learning the things of life. It is true that children don't know everything; they have much to learn. They need to be taught the traditional skills, like math, science, and English. They need to learn a lot of what we know. What we must remember as we teach them is not to take away the gift that they have and we don't—believing. This is not a naïve notion; it is a truth. I have not coached a child in sports who did not think he was going to play professional ball. I have not seen a child doubt his ability to go to space as an astronaut. I have not seen a child develop a plan for something that works perfectly in her mind. What I see when I see a child dream is a boost of confidence and knowledge that I wish I had. One day I realized I could have that back, and my life changed.

For a moment, close your eyes and imagine the dream of a child. Then apply your developed intelligence to his dream. By developed intelligence, I do not mean you should shoot it down and say it could never happen. I mean you should apply your skills to his idea, no matter how silly it may sound. This is the first step to success. Adults need to learn how to dream again.

CHAPTER 5

BUMP YOUR HEAD

Knowing that we need to relearn how to dream, let's think about the process of finding success again. The first step is an old cliché. If you hang around a tattoo parlor, you'll end up with a tattoo. Spend some time with children and get your mind right. Stop thinking you're too busy to take the time. The world won't stop if you take some time to attend to your priorities. I hate to be the one to say this to you, but you are not as important as you like to think you are.

You will be even better at what you do if you're emotionally settled. If you are bound by a job that will not let you develop yourself, makes you feel like a slave, and destroys your self-esteem, it is not worth the money you are making. You sold your happiness for money. You have traded the person you once were for the person you've become. To me, that is a downward spiral. You cannot afford not to take the time to better yourself. Life is right in front of you, but you may not even see it. I'm not suggesting you quit your job; I'm simply suggesting you reevaluate your priorities.

If you do not have children, spend some time with a youth sports programs, or some type of wholesome interaction to see children at their finest. This is where the true education begins. As children play various superheroes and movie characters, the play seems real to them. As they talk to each other, they believe anything they tell each other. It is not because they are easily fooled; it is because they have a broad sense of reality. As we spend time with children and we learn how to laugh again, we also learn how to dream—even dream big if we want.

The next step is to see what type of change we want to make. This is the time we need to ask ourselves what we really want in life. Are we happy? If we are not, what would we need to change? When we do something, we need to do it all the way. Therein lies the difference between those who do and those who wish they could do. If you want to wish for a new sports car, go for it! That is exactly what you need to do. However, if you sit at the bus stop and wait for a guy to walk up and hand you the keys and title, be prepared to wait for more than a long time. Your approach is wrong. Do something about the wish. Make it a reality, a dream come true. That is what needs to happen.

I often become obsessed with things. When I start running, I run too much. It is all I want to do. When my wife and I were first married, we got a dog. It was one of the most memorable times we had together. We would sit in the living room and watch him run his laps around the house. When he passed through the living room from the dining room, we would hear his head bounce along the entire length of the coffee table. *Thunk thunk thunk*, we would hear. When we took him in to the vet for his check up and routine shots, I asked the vet why he would keep doing that. Occasionally, he hit the table so hard that he would spill a drink that was on it. I was curious. His response was one that hit me as a metaphor for the school of life. He said our dog was focusing so much on what he wanted that he did not pay attention to the fact that he was hitting his head. He knew it hurt, but the running was more fun. He chose what he wanted. This is how I get from time to time. My problem is that I get caught up in what I'm doing; I need to be brought back down and rebalance myself. My wife, being the great support she is and knowing me the way she does, will help to get me back to balance. This is the beauty of life. We help each other at all times. None of us is perfect, and we need help from time to time. Sometimes we need it more than other times.

A lot of times in life, we find ourselves doing the same thing over and over and then wonder why there is no change. If we want to incur change, then we must change. When we make a change, we should try not looking for an immediate result. The change needs time for it to present itself. A trend needs to be documented in order for other people to notice or a pattern to display it. At the same time, it needs to be incorporated with the focus of the running dog. We need to want the balance in life so badly that we ignore the bumps on the head. We simply need to redirect our focus.

CHAPTER 6

REMEMBER YOUR ROLE MODELS AND THE REASONS YOU CHOSE THEM

One of my biggest struggles in life is enjoying the present. I'm always too worried about the future. What if I run out of a source of income? What if my house gets cluttered and messy and then company surprises me? What if this? What if that? Then what? I never want to repeat a mistake previously made. That is foolishness to me. What I have learned is this: Sometimes we work hard and other times we play. We find balance. We learn to let the dishes and laundry fall a little behind, but not so much that it is abnormally gross. We divide up duties and set aside times for work. When it is time to play, we play, but not so much that we shirk our responsibilities. My wife understands that sometimes my job keeps me at work for long hours. That is just the way it is. I need to know the difference between reasonable responsibility and obsession. There is a fine line between the two. Sometimes, the answer is as simple as pushing through when I don't feel like it. Other times, it is changing patterns.

Some of the greatest influences to happiness are outlook, perception, self-control, and attitude. If these items are aligned properly, positive self-esteem is the result. When a person has positive self-esteem in place, a positive outlook follows, and success is the result. As I look at my own life, it is more than easy to see that I have made mistakes, in both business and personal aspects. The good news for me is that I was wise enough most of the time to shake it off and do better the next time. I have had a multitude of influences in my life as I grew and matured. I watched these individuals and noticed what they did that made me want to be like them. Before looking at what they did, let me walk you through the things that made them examples to me. Some of my influences are well-known people. Others are just everyday people to most of us. Aside from our Savior and my parents, who will be addressed later, I look at a dear uncle, Uncle Max, who passed on many years ago. He had attributes that I feel many people need more of in life. Above all, he loved God. He also loved his wife, worked hard, and loved people. He was a kind person. He was also a great outdoorsman. He helped me to learn to love the world and nature. I was very young during the years I knew him. He was a pilot during World War II and he loved our country. He taught by example and always made me feel special. As I grew and matured, I remembered the way he treated me. Now that I have my own children, nieces, and nephews, I can only hope I offer to them a taste of what I was blessed with in my youth.

Other influences that have played a major role in my life include Martin Luther, who started the Christian Reformation. He was an amazing individual. He risked his own life for a conviction. That kind of conviction is something many people have lost in our modern world, because they prize material gain over integrity and principle. There is no standing up for us anymore. People settle for being treated badly just so a job is not lost, or a "connection" or fruitful contact is kept. These things are important, but not worth our dignity. Where are the strong spines that formed our country? Let's not go overboard and suggest we operate on short tempers and general disrespect. But we should take a stand when we know a person is stealing, abusing people or situations, or generally being dishonest. These are behaviors that compromise integrity. I have always found it peculiar that the world justifies immoral behavior because the calendar reads "2012." If you are a person who believes in ancient scripture, then you know that morals are not to change with each advent. Who started this misconception? Good morals should be timeless. Overindulgence has always been discouraged. Stealing is never accepted. Honesty is a part of life, not a benefit should we ever encounter it. This has always been true.

As we celebrate Christmas each year, it seems more and more focus is placed on outdoing last year's gifts and celebrations. Does anyone take a moment to find serenity and peace? Or, even better, to find the true spirit of Christmas and at least form a small tear of love and gratitude. My preference these days is to do all of the shopping either really early or really late to avoid the selfish crowds. The fun and magic is slipping. I miss Christmas caroling; I miss singing songs as a family. These are the things that I feel are important to keep as we teach our youth. We need to tell the teens to take the earphones out of their ears and put down the phones. We need to tell the other kids to turn off the video games. We need to restore family values and learn that our greatest strength, any time of year, is at home. I understand that some families are divorced and that children split time. These things happen. Nonetheless, let us not forget the importance of finding the balance that we need to find. The children need to find a feeling of home somewhere and somehow. As adults, I feel it is vital that we become selfless at the right times for the benefit of the ones we claim to put first.

CHAPTER 7

STOP BLAMING OTHER PEOPLE

This generation of "grown-ups" is a peculiar one. This includes me. A lot of us had relatively normal childhoods. We did not necessarily have the Internet or the kinds of portable devices we shower our children with. However, we were on the edge of that horizon. I feel our focus shifted as these things became available. We were a part of the first generation for whom college educations were a little more easily available. We had a more stable economy to deal with. There is no doubt in my mind that we had a lot of things our parents did not. That is not at all a crime; it is blessing for which I will always be grateful, but there are some things I feel we have missed.

As I evaluate the things that have been missed, I keep in mind that they were not necessarily missed on purpose. They were missed because the world is in a place it has never been. In a sense, we are charting the route as we go. One evening after supper my oldest son asked about communism, Hitler, and a general concept of the world before we came along. His mother and I explained to him the ideas that have come about since the French Revolution. We started in the mid 1800s and included the Communist Manifesto. We also discussed Adolf Hitler. It then hit me, as I was talking to him: The world as we know it had only been geographically settled for about 100 years, give or take. For approximately 6,900 years, people had been fighting over power, wealth, and land. As we see the world today, in a clear sense, the same old fights are taking place. Even though they have their own skew to them, they are fundamentally the same conflicts. My point is that our generation has pretty well grown up during the fifty to seventy-five years we have not had to live in the direct fear of losing anything such as land or freedom. We were more focused on settling in and fending for ourselves; we were living our lives. Even though there were a few foreign engagements, the direct impact on our safety did not occur until 9/11.

Evaluating the type of life we have grown to know, and then adding the changes that 9/11 brought, I can easily identify the things we are missing in our lives. The people that raised us directly dealt with World War II—or their parents did. Those before them dealt with the settling of the world. Our generation dealt with affairs not directly related to us. I must first state that military life, losses, and the general angst of war have affected all of our families. I thank our soldiers of all generations. Even though our homeland was not a direct target until recent years, our men and women have gone to protect other lands and homes, therefore securing ours that much more. They are brave; many members of my extended family have been a part of that for many generations, and I hope to continue the legacy. That being said, my point is that our generation grew up not being directly threatened with losing our land or country. Peace times were the result of military service. We were sheltered, protected, and told not to worry for the most part. So we didn't. Now we are adults and we have serious issues on our hands.

We are becoming quick studies, getting involved and learning a lot, but we still will not take a stand because we are too caught up in making money and chasing our selfish desires. We are not worried about the things we should be taking more seriously. We should not blame our parents. They taught us well. I think we simply overlook the issues we see and face today because they were not so serious during our formative years.

CHAPTER 8

YOUR ACTIONS TELL EVERYONE

When I graduated high school, the big push was to go to college to complete my education and secure a living. I do not remember being told to start paying attention to the news and become involved in things that would have a direct impact on our future. I was mostly told to worry about my future. In a sense, we were programmed to be the way we are now. The previous generation, of parents, teachers, counselors, etc. taught us from the things they learned. But due to unavoidable circumstances, their frame of reference was different from ours. They assumed we knew things that they had known in high school, but we had two very different sets of circumstances. We became like dogs running laps and hitting our heads on the table. We missed some of the vital parts—the importance of things like settling down and raising a family, a steady job that allows us a balanced life, and love throughout our lives. These are things that were standard issue in previous generations. They have been replaced by working to the last minute on a holiday weekend. Because it's understood when we occasionally miss school assembly, we take advantage of that fact and electively schedule work to get ahead. Just because our absence is understood and accepted, it does not mean choosing to miss an event is okay. Family and happiness are literally being sold in the world today.

There are many effects of the get-ahead mentality. Aside from missing the things that directly impact our peace, economy, and family, let us consider a few other items. for instance, it is easy to see that obsessively working creates a lot of revenue. The smartphones we have today allow us to create an office out of wherever we are in the world. The car (which is not only wrong, but dangerous), the golf course, anywhere we choose to be can be productive. The fact is that the easier we make business, the busier we get. I'm a victim. I found myself in my office, in front of my computer doing business e-mails from my phone. The direct result is that we are continually setting ourselves up for work. Most people have a hard time letting something go unfinished if they know it can be done. The example is having work e-mails on your phone. If you are taking a day off from work, and you see several e-mails sitting in the folder on your phone, it is human nature to complete them. What's the end result? You ended up working on your day off. What's the fix? Self-control. In Book II of the *Nichomachean Ethics*, Aristotle discusses self-control. He says that exercising self-control should be its own reward. He asserts that exercising self-control and feeling that it was difficult is not exercising self-control. Instead, if we exercise self-control and feel pleased after the experience, the reward is the self-control. That is the idea we need to take when we enjoy life. The other effect of the get-ahead mentality is that we are missing the moment. We are selling out who we are for money, or career-oriented goals. I feel a lot of justifications are being made in the name of need. There is a large difference between working to start up a new business, new job, or expansion, and constantly working toward "progress." If a person is starting a new job or a new business, it is a no-brainer that he will be working more than a lot. But when does this taper off? I strongly believe that spending too much time at work is counterproductive. We need to be fresh to do our best.

If we are settled in our homes, then we are going to be more productive in what we do at work. We are going to enjoy things better on our days off when the office is in order. We are going to sleep better when our finances are arranged properly. We are not going to be cranky because work is bleeding into home and home is bleeding into work, and we get our priorities mixed up. Here are the raw facts: Your employer will function without you. Your family will miss you if you become obsessed with work, and they will eventually emotionally compensate for your being gone. Your employer is not overly concerned with your inability to balance your work life and your home life. No one cares about your priorities more than you. People do what they want above all else. If you don't believe me, let me give you an idea, and you seek the proof. If your spouse sends you with $10.00 to the store to get milk and eggs, and you had something else planned, chances are strong you will comply, regardless of your attitude. If you don't comply, it is because you chose your plans over the grocery store. If you complied, it is most likely out of respect—or you did not want the fight. Either way, you did what you wanted.

CHAPTER 9

GRATITUDE GOES
A LONG WAY

Since we as humans do what we want, we have constant proof of our priorities. We do what we deem most important. If we fake sick at work because we want to sleep in and bum the day away, then we have proven we chose being lazy and unproductive over working to support our lifestyle. If we choose to work excessively until our spouse leaves us, then our priorities are clear. This is the time you need to seriously ask yourself what you really want in life. What makes you happy? Are you afraid to seek it? You are the only one who knows.

I want a happy and full life. I want to wake up and kiss my wife every morning and see my children smiling. I want my finances in order. I also want the opportunity to teach my children the value of work, clean living, and prudence. I am like everyone else. I want the American dream. It is not impossible. I asked myself the same questions. I believe in hard work, I believe in family time, and I believe in saying no on occasion. I also believe in asking for help when it is time to ask. I have been down the road of poverty; I have been down the road of wealth. I could sit here and say they both have their drawbacks, but that is not a true statement. The truth is that how we respond to each is where the drawbacks are found. When I was broke, all I wanted to do was take my family out for a burger and the playground. I could not afford it and I was embarrassed. Retrospectively, I should not have been embarrassed. What I learned was to change my outlook. When I did that, I discovered that a local fast-food place had a Saturday special that fit my tight budget. We had found what we were seeking. In the meantime, I set goals to get to where I wanted to be in life. I set a goal for the next step. My wife stood right behind, me pushing me when she knew I wasn't the guy she married several years ago. She stayed in there. I found the opportunity I needed and I took it. Because of love, attitude, perseverance, and an attitude to face fears to find success, we found what were seeking. We did it with prayer, we did it with faith, and we did it with hope. We said we could when other people said we could not. I learned to believe in myself. I'm grateful for my wife and my family believing in me when I did not believe in myself. That is a direct benefit of success. I was able to have something more than money in my life. What I had is love from my wife, my father, and the rest of my family. They were able to help me when I was down. To me, that is a result of a successful and full life.

There is no struggle or disputation in life that is worth losing someone you love. I have learned that on numerous occasions. There is no greater feeling than being loved. The love of a mother is priceless. My mother passed away in January of 2000. She is missed, but I still feel her love. It carries me through tough times; I try to pass my version of it on to my children. I remember the values she taught me. I remember all that she did for me. I watch my wife with our children. She embodies the love of a mother to our children. There are just some things only a mother can do. For those who were never able to experience those things, I'm so sorry. It was wonderful for me to have it while I did. It is still tough for me to go to my in-laws' house and see my wife and her brother come home to see Mom. I admit I'm a little jealous when I see my wife pick up the phone and call her mom. But above all of my jealousy, far and wide, I'm more than grateful she can still do those things. The pain of death stings deeply and hurts. I'm glad there is hope thereafter. Aside from death, there are also the barriers formed from disputes. We need to eliminate those from our lives. They hurt us. These bring a negative energy that will suck the life from our souls and leave us negative and bitter. The result will be failure in all things, especially happiness. I have been in emotional struggles with my wife, siblings, and parents. They did nothing but cause me harm. As I resolved them, I was grateful that were able to open our feelings and find resolution. What I learned from my experiences is that we will get along if we want to. We must trust, be honest, and set boundaries. We need to find what works and stop recalling the things that caused harm in the past. I have also found that selfless service brings happiness. We serve those we love. We do not buy them with deeds or gifts, but we serve because we love. Over time, the love will be seen and returned, and the balance will be strong.

I am a Christian. I love the Lord Jesus Christ. I love the example he set, as he is my greatest influence and example. I have no problem admitting that there have been many times in my life that I chose not to follow his example. I fell and made bad choices. I feel we all do that sometimes. His example is amazing. He certainly had a perfect balance in life and he led by example. He loved other people; he served everyone. He was able to do things I feel I will never be able to do in my life. Regardless of my inability to emulate him, I still try each day. One thing I'm more than grateful for is the ability to forgive. He made it possible. I figure if he can forgive me and everyone else, who am I to maintain grudges? Who am I to complain? He went through more than I will ever comprehend and he is still the definition of happiness. Because of that, I am able to change my focus in life. This makes me realize the negative energy in my life needs to be eliminated, so I try. I had a teacher in the eighth grade with whom I got in trouble for swearing in class. I responded, sarcastically, that I was sure he never talked like that. He said he had never talked like that since he was in the Marines many years before. I asked him how he was able to stop a habit he had carried for years. His answer was so simple it was profound. He said, "Because I decided I didn't want to anymore." That is the same concept I feel that we as humans can take from the example of the Savior. I will be like him because I decided I want to. I will be happy in my life because I decided I want to. I will spend more time with family, make more money, be more frugal, and succeed more in the allotted time at work because I decided I want to. For the longest time, I thought that religious offerings only included spiritual ones. I think what I was missing was that we need to have a strong spiritual mind-set before we can move forward with other decisions. There are obvious nonspiritual things in the world that are wholesome and good; otherwise all nonspiritual things would be wrong and damaging. We all enjoy a good football game, whether playing or watching, and there are other things to be enjoyed as well. Even though we do not experience a religious enhancement from football, or cycling, or boxing, there is still an opportunity to be a better person through the camaraderie, team building, and many other benefits. These things are for our good. Part of my focus in life is to surround myself with things that better me as a person. I like to be built up, just like anyone else. We all yearn to be loved and adored. We all love to hear nice things said about us. Not all spirited things are immediately spiritual. One of my top goals in my daily experiences is to encounter things that bolster my spirit. I seek a spiritual experience each day in my life. Some days I turn on the radio and rock it out. Other days I keep it turned off. I like to read at night and on breaks. I try to select material that creates a spirit for me to feel. I try to read the scriptures every day, but sometimes I fail.

I find when I am able to do this, my day is always better than a day without. It is a simple process of getting out what you put in.

Jean Paul Sartre wrote, "Man is nothing else but what he makes of himself." This has become one of my favorite quotes. He also made the point that in the world of philosophy, there are constant struggles to prove or disprove the existence of God. His point is that it does not matter what the proof shows. We create what we are, with or without God (based on personal belief). If a person believes in God, then he will allow God in his life enough to assist him in fulfilling his desires and goals. The great point made is that we choose what we do. I made a rule in my house. There are no more negatives. I told my son that I don't want to hear how great other kids are at skateboarding. I want to hear how good he is at skateboarding. His benchmark is against himself, not another. We all have unlimited potential; we just need to overcome the negative energy and push past it to unlock our success. We seem to never attain our desires because we are too clouded by focusing on things we think are in our way. Say it and you will believe it.

Reality is different from negativity. Reality is reality. Here is the difference: "I'm no good at math and it is the only class that keeps me from graduating" versus "Math is the last class I need to take to graduate. I have to work a little harder, but I know I can pass." Many may say the first sentence is real, not negative. It couldn't be more negative. The result is already decided before it has even begun. The second one is real. Having a positive outlook does not eliminate the hard work. If anything in this world is free or easy, I am wary. Seldom is there no catch.

I have already mentioned that I highly doubt there is some wealthy person out there just itching to give some large amount money away. Always be leery. I've been there. It cost me all I had in a material sense. However, I found the good in the experience. It is not a regular occasion that the stock tip of the decade will land in your lap and you will get rich over night. Fine wine comes with time. That is a true statement. Love can be found in a minute, but takes an eternity to grow. It requires attention every day. Respect and trust are earned from every angle. Happiness is a way of life. The common tie with all of those things is that they require daily effort. These are the things we do in life. As I mentioned, people do what they want to do. Therefore, what do we want to do in life? Do we want our love to grow? Do we want a retirement? Do we want to continue to uphold and pursue financial success? None of those things are bad things. They only become bad things when we throw off the balance of moderation. We need money to survive. We need love as we need to give it. We need a future in life. Humans are made to give and receive love. It is a fundamental part of our existence.

CHAPTER 10

MAKE A GOOD LIFE; BE A GOOD PERSON

We, as human beings, need our downtime. We need time alone. We need time to think and reflect, and sometimes just to blow off steam. We become frustrated, we feel crowded, we feel that everyone wants something from us at the same time, and in the midst of all of these things, we have a duty roster four pages long. To make the icing on the cake, it all has to be done two days before payday. That is just the natural cycle of life, so it seems. When we get to feeling like this, it's time for a time-out. When we feel like this, it means we have lost our centers. We are now out of balance. This is the best time to pray, meditate, or go for a walk, a run, or a ride. Although I am indeed a Christian, I love a lot about many other religions. I love the part of the Hindu faith that teaches the connectedness and the unity of the world and nature. All things are connected. There is a need for meditation

41

in religion. Hinduism, like many other religions, teaches the importance of meditation. Through meditation, we can find the connections between things. This is an opportunity to find balance again. We soon learn that all of our responsibilities need to be met, regardless of our attitude. Some days we don't mind doing what we need to do, but on other occasions, we make these things seem tough. The missing link is that the things are easier when we make time for ourselves. We have to keep our batteries charged, too. Just because we are made to give and receive love does not mean that we are not to have some time to collect ourselves and prepare for our daily adventures. It is the same concept of preparing for a test. We spend time studying a little at a time. Then, the day before test, we study more thoroughly than ever. Life is like that. We spend each day preparing for the world, to make each day a good day. If we see a tough day ahead, we should prepare for it. At the conclusion of a tough day, we should then debrief ourselves.

My father, a great man and influence in my life, tells me all the time, "Make it a good day!" rather than "Have a good day." He understands the concept of making your own life. That is what it is all about. He is a great man. He is a great example to me. He shows me it is okay to be sensitive. It is okay to hug your children. It is okay to be in love. All of these things are real to him. He has centered his world on proper balance. We did not grow up wealthy. I knew when I got something big, someone made a sacrifice. While away doing missionary work—self-funded, not organizational—I needed glasses badly. I had no money; my parents were paying for what I was doing, so I relied heavily on them financially. Nonetheless it was important to us that I complete my mission work. On my birthday, I received a birthday card. In it was enough money for a new pair of shoes and glasses, and my loving mother had slipped in a little extra for a drive-thru. I still have the card. On that card was a short note from my parents. I wrote on the back of the card my feelings of gratitude. I never wanted to forget the way I felt when they met my need. I appreciated it. I remember that feeling to this day. I try to recall and re-create that same feeling when I encounter similar blessings in my life. I mention that experience because it was a life-changing experience and changed my perspective in life. It helped me to see the bigger picture. I could name many other times as well—my daughter needed eye surgery, my wife's heart is a little more stable than previously thought, insulin saved my life, and many more. Even bigger moments include my children being born healthy and well. I wake up every day and my love is returned. I can walk and talk. All of those things mean a lot to me. I am grateful for them. I realize those moments, along with anything else I have can be taken away without warning. What then? That is the question for each individual to decide. All I can say is that I recognize that a home, a car, good health, food, and other daily pleasures are not rights; they are not entitlements or expectations. These things are physical blessings. They are blessings I am grateful to have in my life each day.

I want to leave with you a few of my deepest thoughts and inspirations for living. Love the world we have been given. It is the vector for all that we have each day. It offers the air we breathe; it is the source of the food we eat; it is the way we get materials to make the homes we enjoy so much. It is the source of life to us all. Appreciate the beauty of a bird in flight, the majestic scene of mountains, and trees, and all of the bodies of water that give us life. These are gifts to us from the One who made them. Do not take them for granted. Treat the world like you love it. Treat your loved ones like you love them. A little appreciation goes a long way. Remember to say "please" and "thank you." Tell your family you love them, and then show them. Eat meals at the table. Bless your food before eating it. Take your hat off to pray and eat. Show elders respect. Remember the fundamental things in life, like manners, dignity, respect, and eliminating pride. Replace the word "proud" with the word "pleased." Above all, be grateful for all that you have.